# Eddie a... tes...

# At... o



Daniel Nunn

Raintree

Raintree is an imprint of Capstone Global Library Limited, a company incorporated in England and Wales having its registered office at 7 Pilgrim Street, London, EC4V 6LB – Registered company number: 6695582

www.raintreepublishers.co.uk
myorders@raintreepublishers.co.uk


First published in hardback in 2014
Paperback edition first published in 2015


Edited by Rebecca Rissman, Daniel Nunn, and Catherine Veitch
Designed by Jo Hinton-Malivoire
Original illustrations © Capstone Global Library Ltd 2013
Illustrations by Steve Walker
Picture research by Ruth Blair
Production by Sophia Argyris
Originated by Capstone Global Library Ltd
Printed and bound in China by Leo Paper Products Ltd

ISBN 978 1 406 26310 7 (hardback)
17 16 15 14 13
10 9 8 7 6 5 4 3 2 1

ISBN 978 1 406 26315 2 (paperback)
18 17 16 15 14
10 9 8 7 6 5 4 3 2 1

**British Library Cataloguing in Publication Data**
A full catalogue record for this book is available from the British Library.

**Acknowledgements**
We would like to thank the following for permission to reproduce photographs: Shutterstock pp. 7t (© Elnur), 7m (© Gnilenkov Aleksey), 7b (© Dudarev Mikhail), 8 (© Fukuoka Irina), 9tl (© paytai), 9tr (© Four Oaks), 9bl (© Martin Dallaire), 9br (© Juriah Mosin), 10 (© Shchipkova Elena), 11 (© IrinaK), 12 (© Pablo77), 13 (© Roman Teteruk), 14b (© Stu Porter), 14tl (© Africa Studio), 15 (© Jiri Hera), 16 (© Christian Musat), 17 (© Jason Mintzer), 18 (© Jason Prince), 19 (© Dhoxax), 20 (© Jan Martin Will), 21 (© Ivan Pavlov), 22 (© Karel Gallas), 23l (© Elena Larina), 23r (© Pal Teravagimov).

Cover photograph of a Lar gibbon reproduced with permission of Shutterstock (© Palo_ok).

Every effort has been made to contact copyright holders of any material reproduced in this book. Any omissions will be rectified in subsequent printings if notice is given to the publisher.

# Contents

# Meet Eddie and Ellie

This is Eddie the Elephant.

This is his friend, Ellie the Elephant.

Eddie and Ellie don't always agree.

# Opposites

Everything that Eddie likes...
Ellie likes the opposite!

Opposites are completely different from each other.

Eddie only likes **WET** weather.

But Ellie only likes **DRY** weather!
My goodness, what funny elephants!

# A visit to the zoo

Today, Eddie and Ellie are going to the zoo.

Have you ever been to a zoo?

# Big and small

Eddie likes big animals at the zoo.
Polar bears are **BIG**.

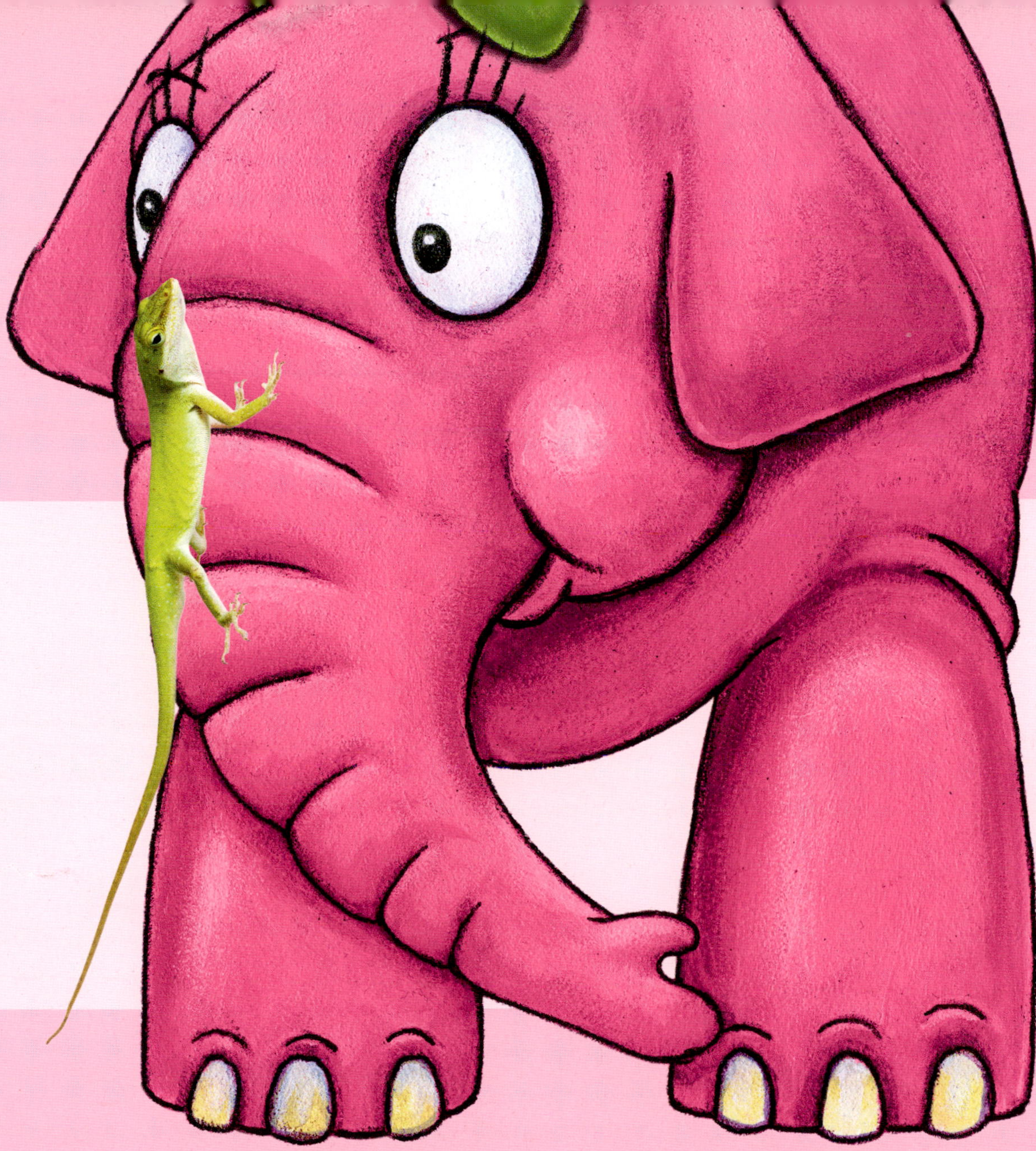

Ellie likes small animals at the zoo.

Lizards are **SMALL**.

# Loud and quiet

Eddie likes loud animals at the zoo. This lion has a **LOUD** roar.

Ellie likes quiet animals at the zoo.
This chameleon is **QUIET**.

# Fast and slow

Eddie likes fast animals at the zoo.
This cheetah is **FAST**.

Ellie likes slow animals at the zoo.
This giant tortoise is **SLOW**.

# Tall and short

Eddie likes tall animals at the zoo.

This giraffe is **TALL**.

Ellie likes short animals at the zoo.

This toad is **SHORT**.

# Heavy and light

Eddie likes heavy animals at the zoo.

This rhinoceros is **HEAVY**.

Ellie likes light animals at the zoo.

This lemur is **LIGHT**.

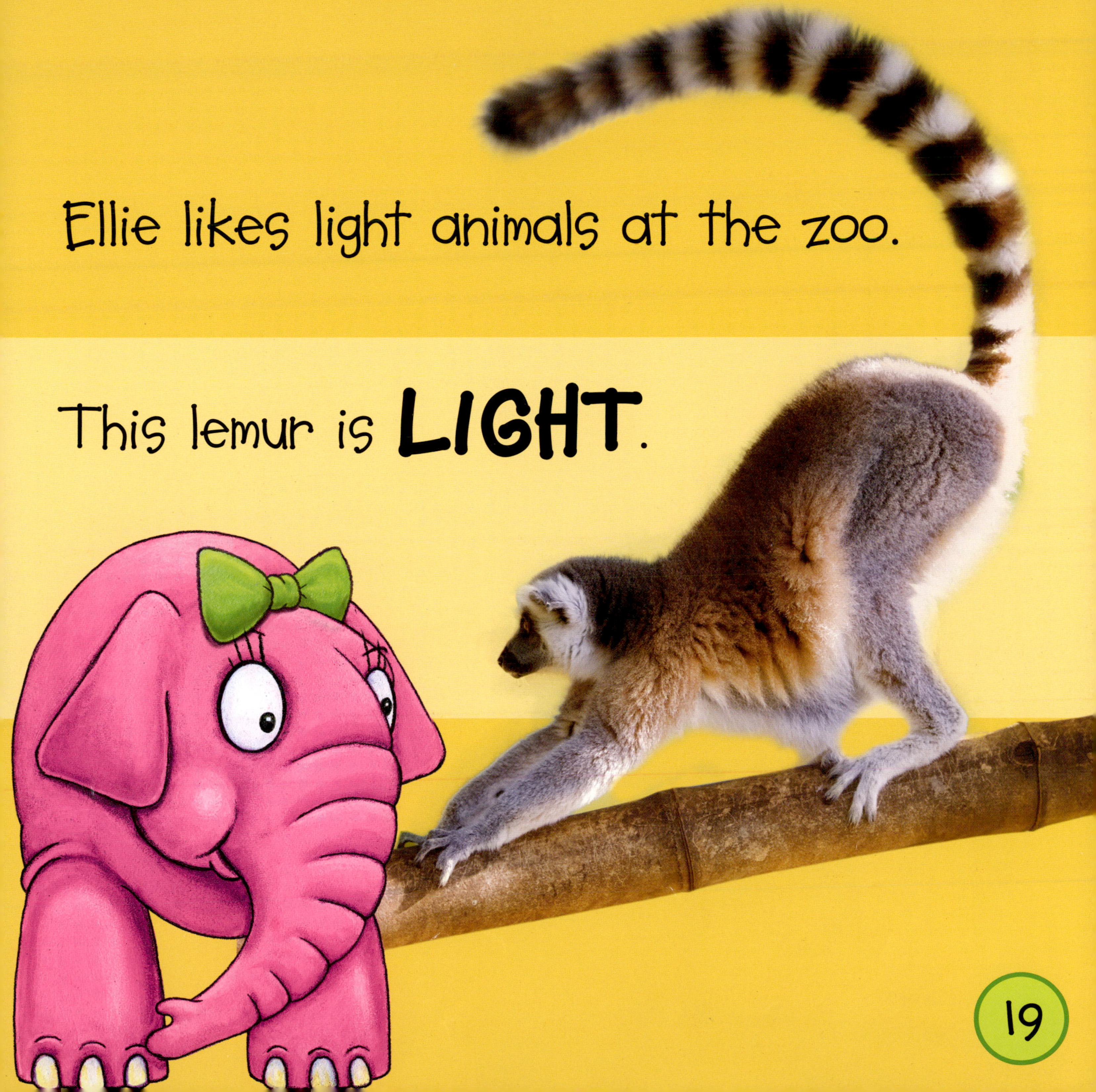

# Cold and hot

Eddie likes animals from cold places.

These penguins are from freezing **COLD** Antarctica.

Ellie likes animals from hot places.
This camel is from the scorching
**HOT** Sahara Desert!

# Can you work it out?

Eddie likes animals with
**ROUGH** skin.

Do you think Ellie likes animals with **ROUGH** skin, or animals with **SMOOTH** skin?

# Opposites quiz

How many of these words do you know the opposites for?

**happy**

**awake**

**narrow**

## Answers

**Answer to question on page 23**

Ellie likes animals with smooth skin.

**Answers to quiz**

The opposite of happy is sad.

The opposite of narrow is wide.

The opposite of awake is asleep.